# CHRISTMAS TIME IS HERE

## 7 Arrangements for Brass Quintet

**Selections from The Canadian Brass CD
(Opening Day Entertainment Group)**

ISBN 978-1-4803-6038-9

## THE CANADIAN BRASS

DISTRIBUTED BY

### HAL•LEONARD® CORPORATION

7777 W. BLUEMOUND RD. P.O. BOX 13819 MILWAUKEE, WI 53213

www.canadianbrass.com
www.halleonard.com

# CONTENTS

Tuba

# ANGEL CHOIR AND THE TRUMPETER

Music and Lyrics by Chris Dedrick
Adapted by Chris Coletti

Tuba

# BACH'S BELLS

Inspired by Bach's BWV 29 and
Leontovych's CAROL OF THE BELLS

Chris Coletti

# MY LITTLE DRUM

By Vince Guaraldi
Arranged and adapted by Brandon Ridenour

# HARK, THE HERALD ANGELS SING

Felix Mendelssohn
Arranged by Brandon Ridenour

# O TANNENBAUM

Traditional
Arranged by Vince Guaraldi
Adapted by Brandon Ridenour

# SKATING

By Vince Guaraldi
Arranged by Brandon Ridenour

# WHAT CHILD IS THIS?

Traditional
Arranged and adapted by Brandon Ridenour

81

86

91

97

102

107

112

117